SCHOLASTIC

BOB® BOOKS

Developing Readers

Workbook

Word Families (K-1)

Ask for Bob Books® at your local bookstore, or visit www.bobbooks.com.

ISBN 978-93-5471-665-2

Printed in India

This reprint edition, August 2025

Bob Books: Word Families
Workbook

Floppy Mop

Use **cat**, **sat**, and **is** to complete each sentence. Then read the story and colour each picture.

Mop was Tom's pal.

Tom ________ on Mop.

Jack was a ________.

Zack was a rat.

Mop ran after Jack and Zack.

Mop and Tom ________.

Colour Tom, Mop, Jack, and Zack.
Who sat on Mop? ____________

Mop was Tom's pal.

Zack ran. Jack ran after Zack.

Floppy Mop

Circle and write the correct word.

pal gal

Zack Sack

happy floppy

stop flop

cap nap

Tom Mom

Find and colour the hidden word. Then draw a line to the matching picture.

Floppy Mop

Find the sight words and colour them to match the key below. Count how many you found.

a	was	said	come	after

Mop was a big dog.

Mop was Tom's pal.

"Come, Mop," said Tom.

Zack was a rat.

Jack was a cat.

Jack ran after Zack.

Mop ran after Jack and Zack.

I found ______ **"was"** words.

I found ______ **"after"** words.

Circle and write the correct word to match the picture.

Mop was a big dog.

(big dig)

_______ was a cat.

(Sack Jack)

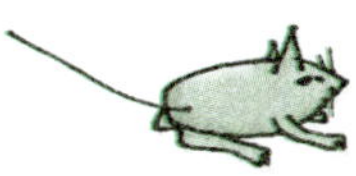

_______ was a rat.

(Pack Zack)

Mop was _______ pal.

(Tom's Mom's)

Mop was a _______ dog.

(sloppy floppy)

Floppy Mop

Read, say, and write the words.

pal  pal

nap 

Tom 

floppy 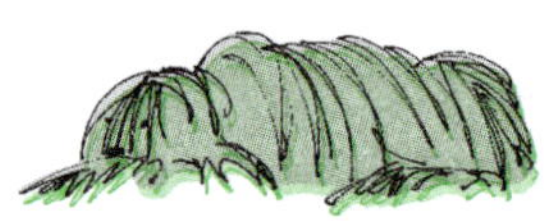

Zack 

stop 

Write the words in the correct order to make the sentences.

was Jack cat. a

Jack

sat Mop. on Tom

Tom's was pal. Mop

Lolly-Pops

Colour the lolly-pops.
How many lolly-pops do you see? __________

Use **shop** and **was** to complete each sentence.
Then read the story and colour each picture.

Polly ______ a jolly bird.

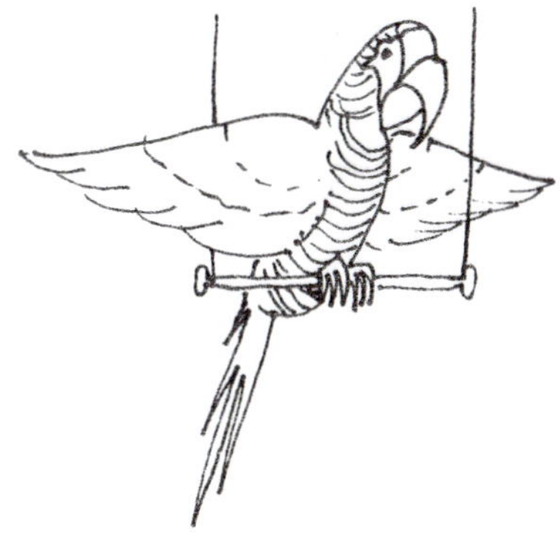

Polly flapped. Polly bobbed.

Polly sat on Dolly.

Dolly and Jon went to a ________.

The ________ had lolly-pops.

Dolly and Jon got lolly-pops.

Lolly-Pops

Circle and write the correct word.

flap snap

stop shop

Polly Dolly

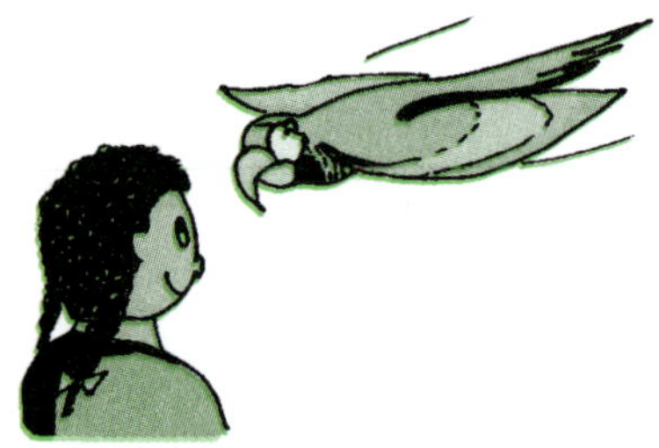

new flew

molly lolly-pop

Dolly jolly

Find and colour the hidden word. Then draw a line to the matching picture.

y f l a p • • 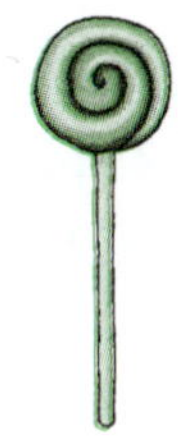

P o l l y x • • 

g l o l l y - p o p • • 

s h o p c • • 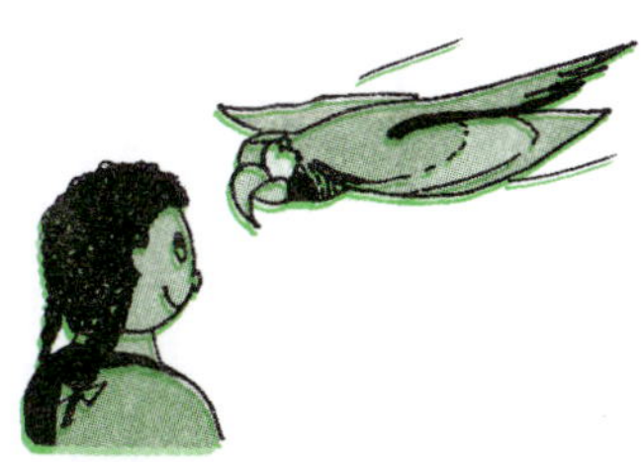

i D o l l y • • 

f l e w j • • 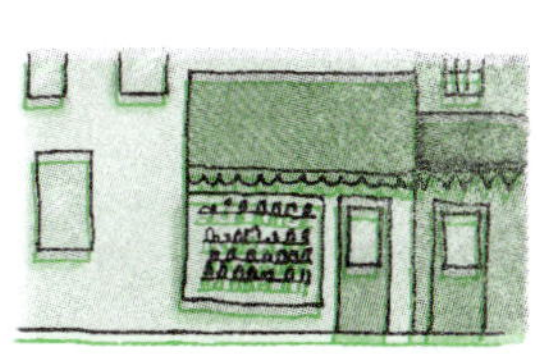

Lolly-Pops

Find the sight words and colour them using the key below. Count how many you found.

to	wants	was	said	a

Polly was a jolly bird.

"Hello, Polly," said Jon.

Polly flew to Dolly.

Dolly and Jon went to a shop.

"Polly wants a lolly-pop."

"Yum, yum!" said Polly.

I found ______ **"to"** words.

I found ______ **"said"** words.

Circle and write the correct word to match the picture.

The ________ had lolly-pops.

(shop   stop)

Dolly and ________ went to a shop.

(Jon   Jin)

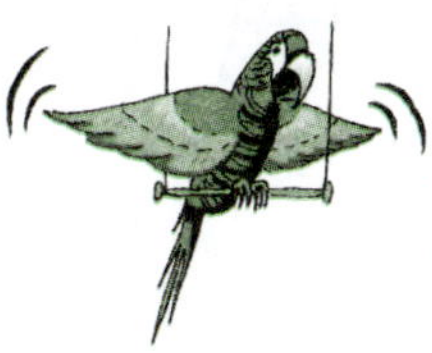

Polly ________ .

(flapped   snapped)

Dolly had ________ pennies.

(ten   men)

"Yum, ________ , ________ !" said Dolly.

(mum   yum)

Lolly-Pops

Write the words in the correct order to make the sentences.

flew Dolly. Polly to

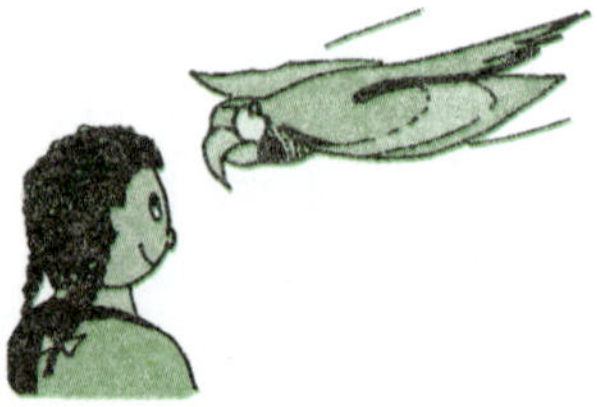

sat Polly Dolly. on

six Jon pennies. had

Read, say, and write the words.

flap

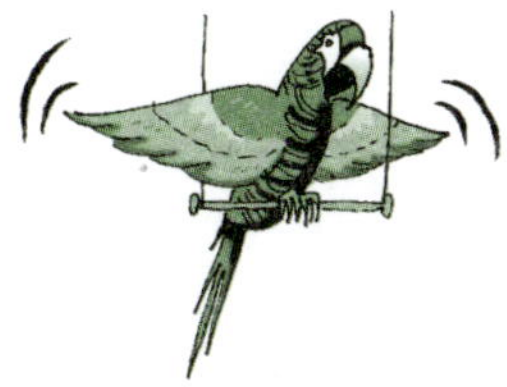

flap

Polly

lolly-pop

shop

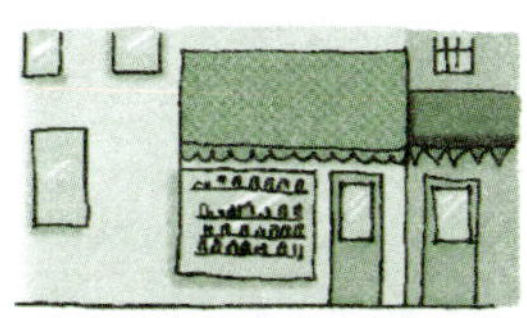

Dolly

flew

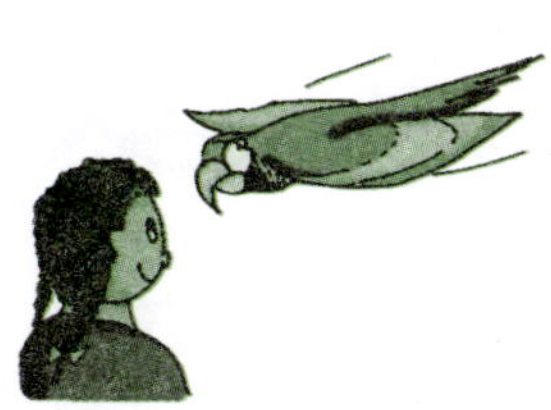

Frogs

Colour the polliwogs and frogs.
How many polliwogs do you see? ________

Polliwogs

Frogs

Use **frogs**, **jump**, and **big** to complete each sentence. Then read the story and colour each picture.

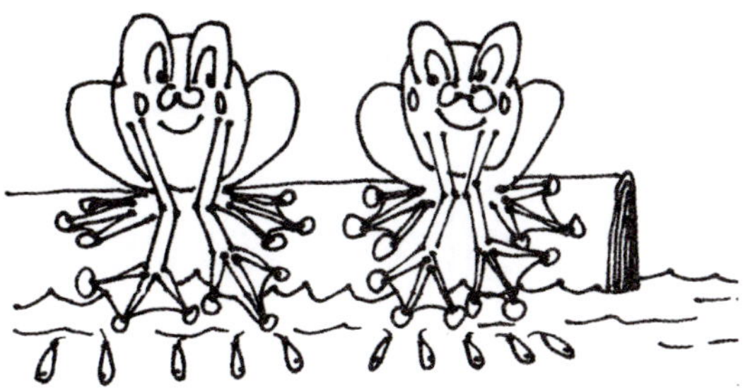

Ten polliwogs swam in the pond.

The bird was ________ and tall.

The bird saw the polliwogs and ________.

"Jump! Hide!" said Papa.

"________! Dive!" said Mama.

The frogs went under a log.

Frogs

Circle and write the correct word.

pond bond

slim swim

third bird

wonder under

small tall

frog hog

Find and colour the hidden word. Then draw a line to the matching picture.

w p o n d	
k f r o g	
u n d e r q	
m s w i m	
b i r d d	
c t a l l	

Frogs

Find the sight words and colour them to match the key below. Count how many you found.

bird	a	went	the	was

A bird was in the pond.

The bird was big and tall.

The polliwogs went under a log.

The frogs went under a log.

For dinner the bird had a big hot dog.

I found ______ "**went**" words.

I found ______ "**the**" words.

Circle and write the correct word to match the picture.

The bird was ______ and tall.

(big pig)

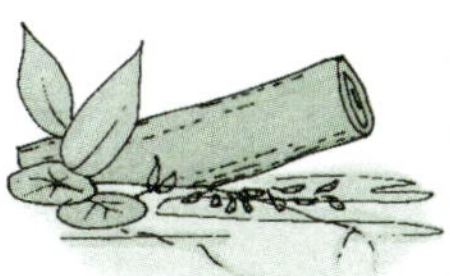

The polliwogs ______ under a log.

(bent went)

The frogs went under a ______.

(hog log)

______! Hide!

(Pump Jump)

The bird saw the polliwogs and ______.

(frogs smogs)

Frogs

Read, say, and write the words.

pond  pond

bird 

under 

frog 

swim 

tall 

Put the words in the correct order to make a sentence.

the | bird | The | saw | frogs.

tall. | The | was | bird

bird | the | was | pond. | A | in

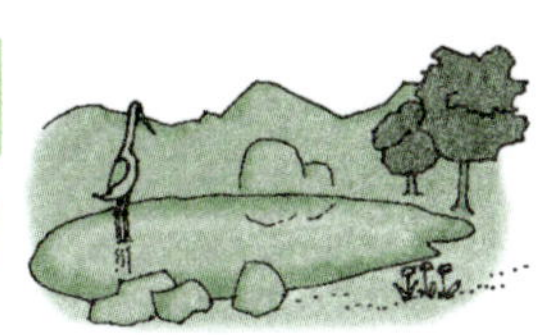

The Red Car

Colour the kids.
Who has a red cap? ________

The Red Car

Carl Mark Barb

Use **start** and **star** to complete the sentences.
Then read the story and colour each picture.

Barb had a red car.

The car was a ________.

The red car did not ________.

Mark hopped out.
Carl hopped out.

The car started.

Barb, Mark, and Carl sped off in the red car.

The Red Car

Circle and write the correct word.

push cash

Bark Barb

car far

star jar

mart smart

start part

Find and colour the hidden word. Then draw a line to the matching picture.

l p u s h 

c a r p 

f s t a r 

t s m a r t 

B a r b b 

s t a r t q 

The Red Car

Find and colour the sight words.
Count how many you found.

will	we	out	was	said

The red car was a star.

Mark hopped out.

Carl hopped out.

"We will push the car," said Mark and Carl.

"Smart!" said Barb.

I found ______ **"out"** words.

I found ______ **"said"** words.

Circle and write the correct word to match the picture.

Barb had a ________ car.

(red bed)

The car ________.

(man ran)

Barb sat in the ________.

(star car)

The car did not ________.

(start smart)

"Hop in, Mark.

________ in, Carl," said Barb.

(Hop Pop)

The Red Car

Put the words in the correct order to make a sentence.

out. Mark hopped

a The star. car was

car started. The

Read, say, and write the words.

push

push

star

car

start

Barb

smart

Summer

Colour the sun.
Colour the tree.
What is your favorite season? ____________

summer fall winter spring

Use **pond** and **hot** to complete the sentences.
Then read the story and colour each picture.

It was ________.

Molly and Mom went to the ________.

Ducks swam in the pond.
Fish swam in the pond.

Molly put her toes in the pond.

Molly and Mom jumped into the pond.

Molly and Mom sat in the pond.
The sun was ________, but the pond was not.

Summer

Use a word from the word bank to fill in the boxes.

Word Bank

Molly red duck fish hot Mom

h o t

Write the letters from the coloured boxes.

Find and colour the hidden word. Then draw a line to the matching picture.

t d u c k ● ● 

f i s h r ● ● 

y M o l l y ● ● 

M o m x ● ● 

h o t b ● ● 

t o e s k ● ● 

Summer

Colour the bubbles with the word "**her**" red.
Colour the bubbles with the word "**into**" blue.
Colour the bubbles with the word "**put**" orange.
Use these words to finish the sentences.

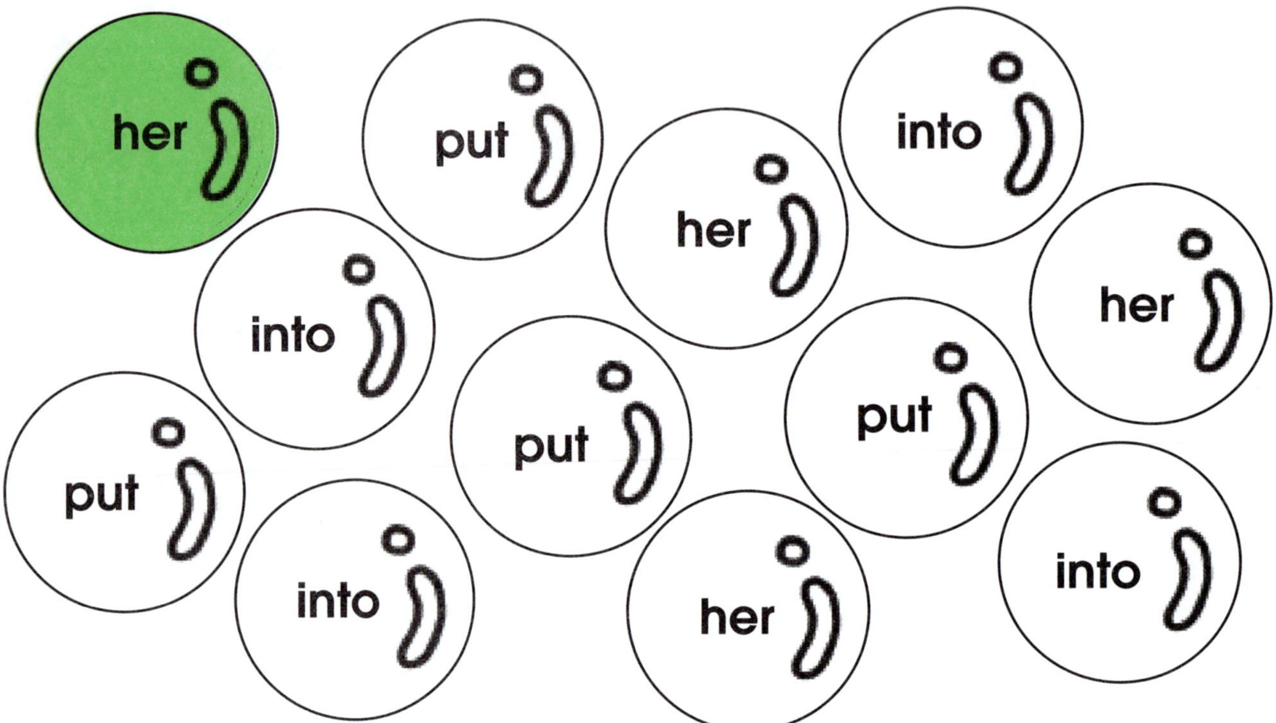

Mom ______ her hands in the pond.

Molly put ______ toes in the pond.

Molly and Mom jumped ______ the pond.

Circle and write the correct word to match the picture.

It was __________.

(pop hot)

Molly had a big __________.

(cat hat)

__________ swam in the pond.

(Ducks Trucks)

Molly and __________ sat in the pond.

(Tom Mom)

Molly and Mom __________.

(jumped pumped)

Summer

Put the words in the correct order to make the sentences.

was hot It

_ _   _ _ _   h _ _ .

pond sat the They in

_ _ _ _   s _ _   _ _

t _ _   _ _ _ _ .

swam the Fish in pond

_ _ _ _   s _ _ _   _ _

_ _ _   p _ _ _ .

Read, say, and write the words.

Molly  Molly

toes 

duck 

fish 

hot 

Mom 

Kittens

Colour the kittens.
How many kittens do you see? ____________
What is your favorite pet? ____________

dog cat bird hamster fish horse

Use **bed** and **luck** to complete the sentences.
Then read the story and colour each picture.

Jill met a big cat.

Jill was sad.
Cat was sad.

"What is the matter?"
said Jim.

"The cat had bad
________," said Jill.

"I saw six kittens
in my ________," said Bill.

The cat was happy.

Kittens

Use a word from the word bank to fill in the boxes.

Word Bank

kittens call ran six happy luck

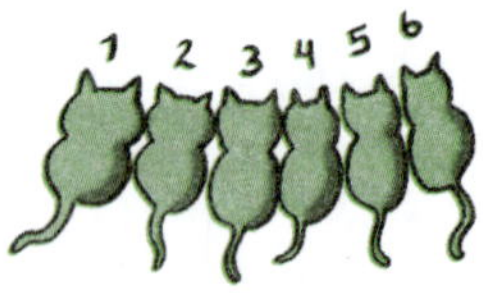

Write the letters from the coloured boxes.

Find and colour the hidden word. Then draw a line to the matching picture.

k i t t e n s r

n c a l l

r a n c

s i x l

y h a p p y

p l u c k

Kittens

Colour the cats with the word "**her**" purple.
Colour the cats with the word "**are**" yellow.
Colour the cats with the word "**saw**" blue.
Use these words to finish the sentences.

The cat has lost ______ kittens.

The cat and Jill and Jim ______ sad.

"I ______ six kittens in my bed," said Bill.

Circle and write the correct word to match the picture.

Jill met a ________ cat.

(big dig)

Jill and Cat were ________.

(sad mad)

"The cat had ________ luck," said Jill.

(dad bad)

"I saw ________ kittens in my bed," said Bill.

(mix six)

Jill and Jim and Cat ran to Bill's ________.

(bed red)

Kittens

Put the words in the correct order to make the sentences.

big a met Jill cat

_ _ _ _   _ _ _   _   b _ _

_ _ _.

sad Jill was

_ _ _ _   _ _ _   s _ _.

was The happy cat

_ _ _   _ _ t   _ _ _

_ _ _ _ _.

Read, say, and write the words.

kittens  kittens

call 

ran 

six 

happy 

luck 

Funny Bunny

Colour the bunnies.
What are they doing? ________

Funny Bunny

Use **run**, **fox**, and **luck** to complete the sentences. Then read the story and colour each picture.

Tup and Tip had fun.

Lox the ________ was hungry.

"The fox is cunning. The fox wants us for supper. ________!" said Tup.

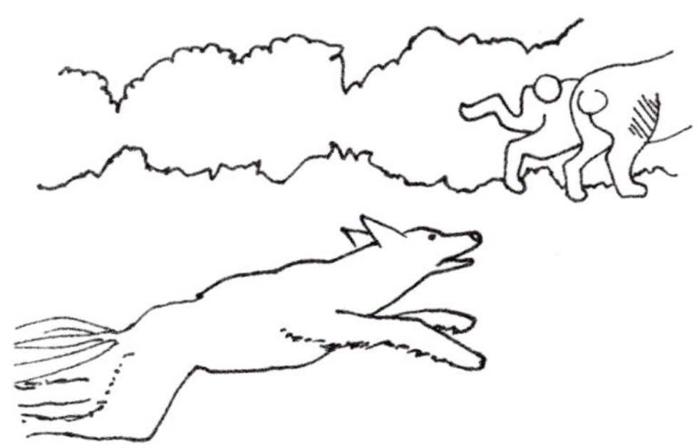

But the fox ran fast.

The fox was out of ________.

Tip and Tup had carrots and turnips for supper.

Funny Bunny

Use a word from the word bank to fill in the boxes.

Word Bank

run up down fox fun fast

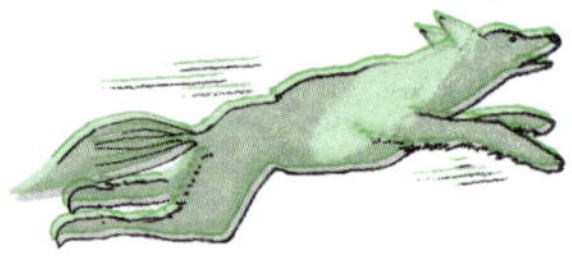

Write the letters from the coloured boxes.

Find and colour the hidden word. Then draw a line to the matching picture.

p r u n

i u p j

d o w n f

k f o x

b f u n l

f a s t w

Funny Bunny

Colour the balls with the word "**did**" orange.
Colour the balls with the word "**out**" green.
Colour the balls with the word "**went**" red.
Use these words to finish the sentences.

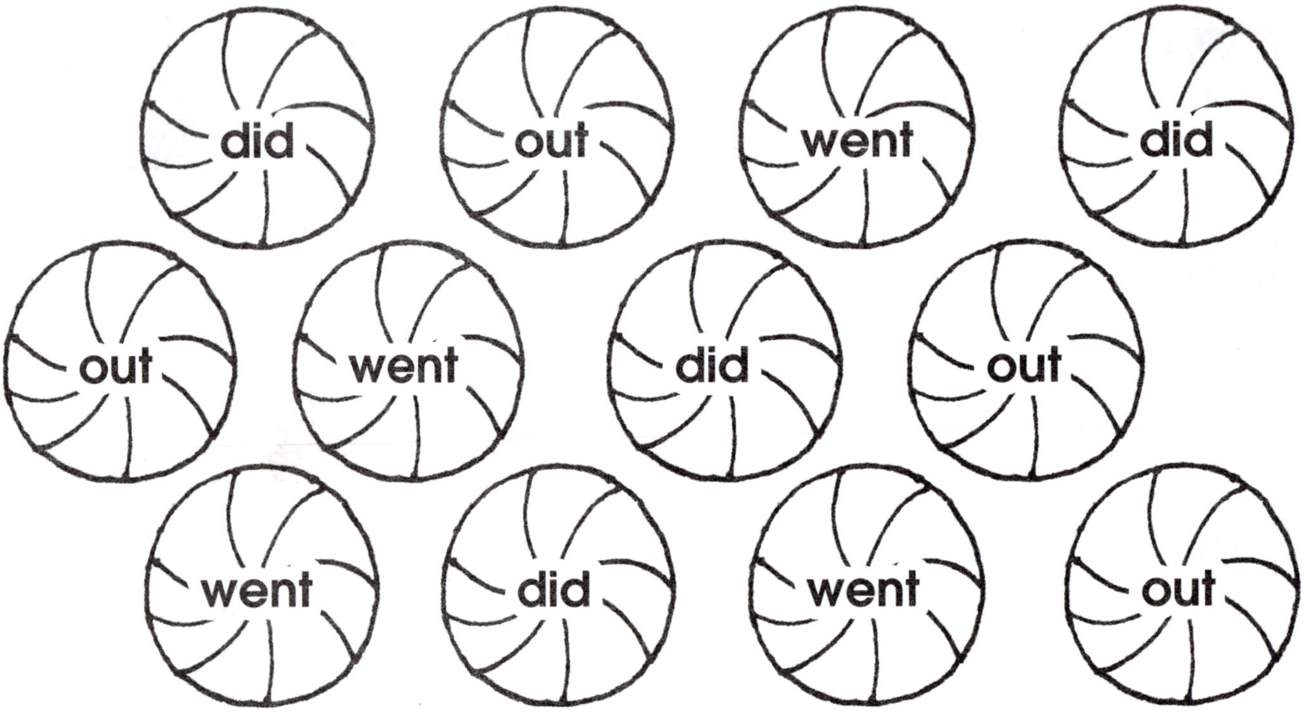

Tup and Tip ______ stunts.

"Puff, puff, puff," ______ the fox.

The fox was ______ of luck.

Circle and write the correct word to match the picture.

Tup and ______ did stunts.

(Tip   Jip)

Tup and Tip had ______.

(fun   sun)

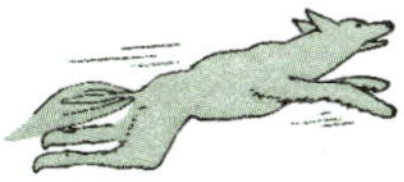

The fox ______ fast.

(ran   fan)

The ______ was out of luck.

(box   fox)

______ and Tup had carrots and turnips for supper.

(Jip   Tip)

Funny Bunny

Put the words in the correct order to make the sentences.

fox ran The fast

_ _ _   f _ _   _ _ _

_ _ _ _.

hungry The fox was

_ _ _   _ _ _   w _ _

_ _ _ _ _ _.

jumped down Tup

_ _ _   _ u _ _ _ _

_ _ _ _.

Read, say, and write the words.

run  run

up 

down 

fox 

fun 

fast 

Bed Bugs

Colour the clock.
What time is it? ________

Use **clock**, **end**, and **up** to complete the sentences. Then read the story and colour each picture.

The ________ struck ten.

Meg and Fred were sent to bed.

Fred jumped ________.

Papa was upset. Mama was upset.

Meg and Fred jumped and the big bed fell.

That was the ________ of jumping on the bed.

Bed Bugs

Use a word from the word bank to fill in the boxes.

Word Bank

bend Fred head upset rest clock

Write the letters from the coloured boxes.

Find and colour the hidden word. Then draw a line to the matching picture.

b e n d w

a f r e d

v h e a d

r e s t d

c l o c k a

Bed Bugs

Colour the beds with the word "**on**" purple.
Colour the beds with the word "**down**" green.
Colour the beds with the word "**all**" red.
Use these words to finish the sentences.

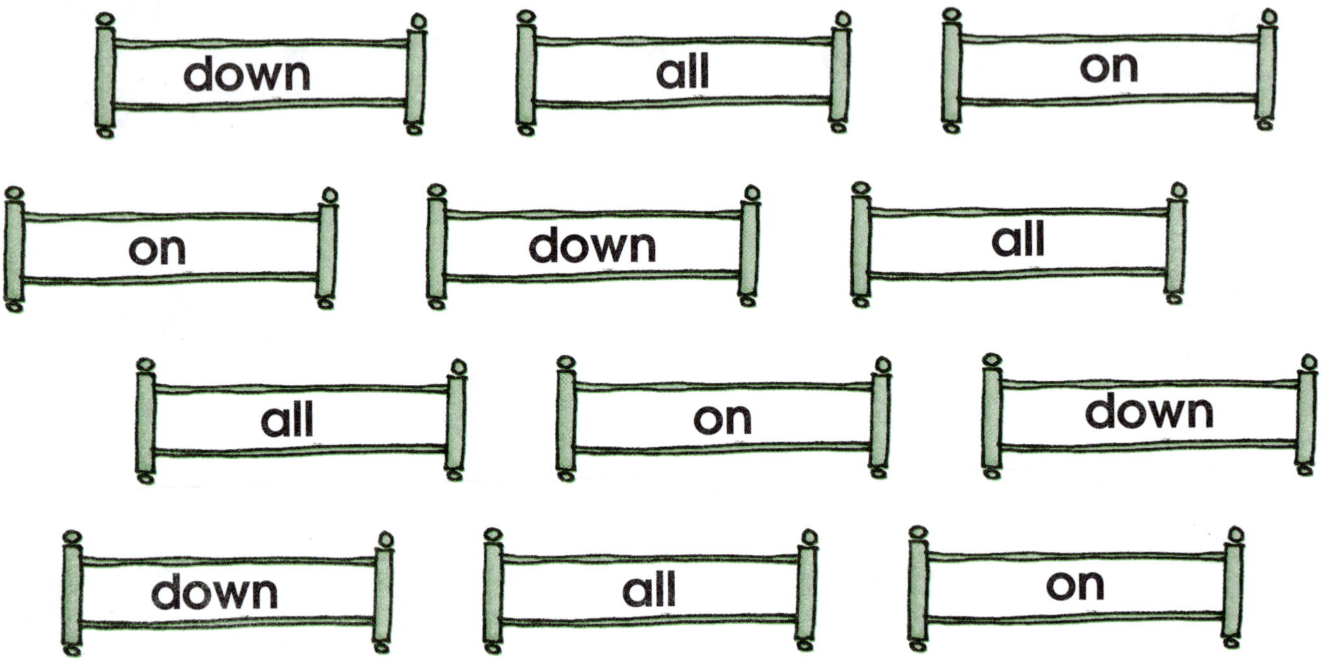

Fred and Meg jumped
______ the bed.

Meg jumped ______ .

Papa said,
"Hush ______ that fuss."

Circle and write the correct word to match the picture.

The ________ struck ten.

(clock   block)

________ jumped up.

(Sled   Fred)

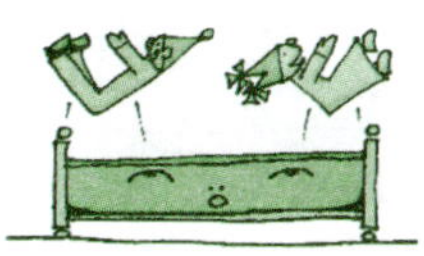

Fred felt the bed ________.

(bend   send)

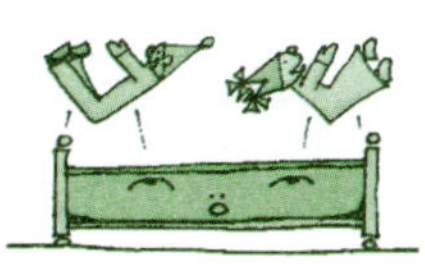

Meg felt the bed ________.

(bump   pump)

Papa said, "Hush all that ________."

(muss   fuss)

Bed Bugs

Put the words in the correct order to make the sentences.

ten struck The clock

_ _ _ c _ _ _ _

_ _ _ _ _ _ _ _ _ .

jumped Fred up

_ r _ _ _ _ _ _ _ _ _ _ .

was upset Papa

_ _ _ _ _ _ _ u _ _ _ _ _ .

Read, say, and write the words.

bend  bend

Fred 

head 

upset 

rest 

clock 

connect the smiley faces in the box so that you can reach the fruit.

Find 10 farm animals and 10 zoo animals in the picture below. Circle them with different colour pencils.

Help baby elephant reach mumma elephant safely through the maze!

complete the figure by joining the dots.

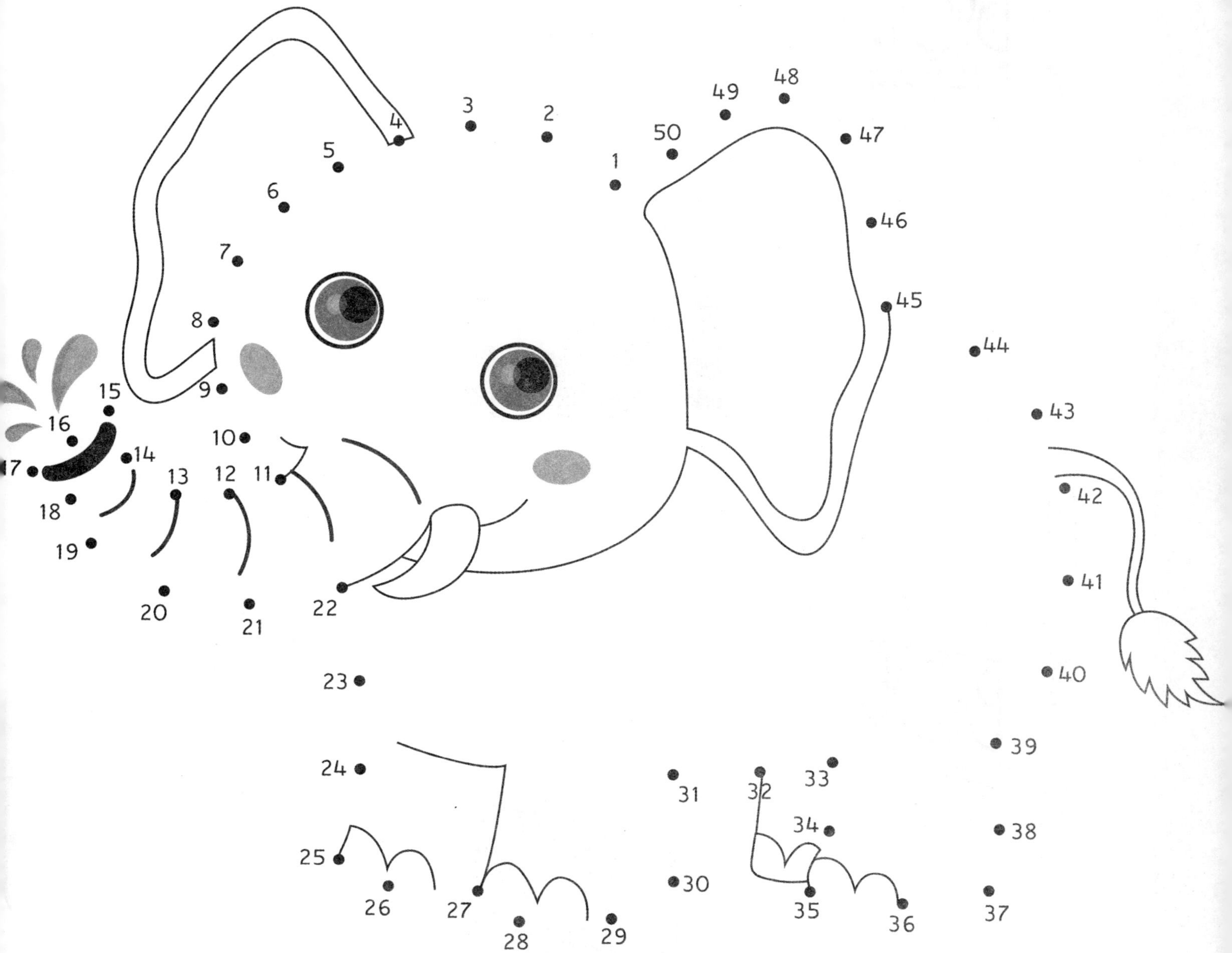

STAGE 2: EMERGING READER
BOB BOOKS
SET 2
Advancing Beginners
SCHOLASTIC

STAGE 1: STARTING TO READ
BOB BOOKS
SET 1
SCHOLASTIC

STAGE 3: DEVELOPING READER
BOB BOOKS
SET 3
Word Families
SCHOLASTIC

BOB BOOKS®

STAGE 3: DEVELOPING READER
BOB BOOKS
SET 4
Complex Words
SCHOLASTIC

STAGE 1: STARTING TO READ
BOB BOOKS
More Beginning Readers
SCHOLASTIC

STAGE 3: DEVELOPING READER
BOB BOOKS
SET 5
Long Vowels
SCHOLASTIC